Why? Why? Why?

Dear friend,
The loss of malaika,
our precious baby girl
is painfully unbearable.
Hope these poems can
bring some way of expressi
those emotions & bring
some relief.
♡ SC

GEORGIA A. COCKERHAM

ISBN: 0989240819
ISBN 9780989240819

Original Watercolor paintings
By Georgia Cockerham

Photo of Zach in truck by Jay Watson,
Taken from book *Broken Down Heroes* by Jay Watson

Back cover photos by Bruce Cockerham

Additional Books by Georgia Cockerham

Wildlife Friends: Northwest Coast

colorandwordsbygeorgia@gmail.com
www.colorandwordsbygeorgia.com

Contents

I wish to thank my husband, Bruce, for his kind editorials and patience with me during the years I put my feelings onto paper and then struggled emotionally with whether to publish and expose my deepest thoughts on a grief journey to hell and back. I am grateful to Zach's widow, Jessica, his brother Aaron, and Aaron's wife, Patricia, for their love and support. Zach will always be remembered with love and respect.

Preface

Zachary Owen Ward died May 25, 2003, when a motorist ran a red light, crossing in front of Zach as he entered an intersection on a motorcycle. He was twenty-seven years old and the younger of my two sons.

I had written poetry for decades, but my writing stopped when Zach died. It took years before I could write again, and when I finally picked up my pen, the dam broke, allowing my pain to gush out onto paper and into, first, my poems and then my paintings.

Being a bereaved parent is very isolating due to the basic inability of the general public to understand. I found great healing in both learning about the survival stories of others and, as I healed, providing hope to those who were also suffering. This healing process has taken place primarily through an organization called The Compassionate Friends, Inc. (TCF), a nonprofit self-help bereavement group for those who have suffered the death of a son, daughter, grandchild, or sibling. In addition to serving five years on the TCF national board of directors, I currently volunteer in my eleventh year overseeing the Northwest Coast Chapter formed by my husband and me after Zach's death. Monthly meetings are the primary focus of the chapter, and as meeting facilitator I've met, listened to, and spoken with hundreds of bereaved individuals initially lost in the dark fog of grief, not knowing if they would survive. Reference in my poetry to helping others has been through my TCF experience.

My poems are arranged to expose my healing over time as I fought back the darkness and isolation while adapting to the new world in which I lived, a world in which I could no longer experience my son Zach. I offer my writings as opportunities of hope and healing to others.

EARLY GRIEF

WHY? WHY? WHY?

So many times I screamed at Thee,
What have you done and Why?
Rapists and murderers walk this earth
Why'd my child have to die?

Why I'm alive to think and write
The wrongs of my child's death,
When it's me you should have called
Never taking his last breath.

I've tried but cannot comprehend
Ending a life so young.
With much of him still left to give,
His journey just begun.

Not knowing *Why* has haunted me,
Acceptance I'll not find.
The lurking question hides and waits
In shadows of my mind.

Why? Why? Why?

REMEMBERING ZACH
(in early grief)

~~~~~~~~~~~~~~~~~~~~~~~~~~~~~~

Look at you, Zach, my new baby boy,
Big Blue eyes, giving so much joy.
You made complete our family plan,
Giving me much more to understand.

Look at you, Zach, my growing son,
Showing keen wit and imagination.
You'd play Daniel Boone, exploring new lands.
Giving me much more to understand.

Look at you, Zach, others following you,
An exemplary marine in all that you do!
So proud to know I had a hand.
Giving me much more to understand.

Look at you, Zach, as you say "I do."
With lover and friend in love with you, too.
You've grown into such an honorable man.
Giving me much more to understand.

Look at you, Zach. But I couldn't they said.
Motorcycle down, great trauma to head.
Broken, I'm told to start over again.
Life is too much. Can't comprehend.

FORGIVING

~~~~~~~~~~~~~~~~

The word *forgive* so very strong.
Unable to do so, for many, is wrong.

He drove the car that took my son's life,
Leaving a widow where had been a wife.

Took a man's brother, lives just begun.
Stole the uncle to daughters and son.

Sat in his car, though he could see
Man down in the street, he just let him be.

Destroyed many lives, countless tears shed
From the moment I learned my child was dead.

Forgive is a strong word and follows a course
Led by he in the wrong who must first show remorse.

WHY HE'S GONE

How is it that everyone knows
Why my child died so young?
One says "his work was finished here,"
Another "his song was sung."

"God needed another angel,"
"He picks the best, my dear."
His broken family will tell all
The greater need was here.

"Give him up," "let him go home,"
"Not yours to keep," "he was on loan."
Part of some great experiment?
To right man's wrongs? Angel for rent?

SUDDEN DEATH

Sudden death is so unkind,
It leaves no time to say
Good-bye, I love you, see you soon,
Next time can you stay?

What do I do with all the thoughts
I wanted to express?
The apologies and compliments
And questions not addressed?

There's no one else to take your place
I need to talk with you.
So much I waited to explain,
There simply was no clue.

Impossible to sort out,
No words that can express,
Your leaving here so suddenly
Has left my mind a mess.

MENTION HIS NAME

We sat around the table
Struggling for what to say,
You talk of this and that
Never mentioning his name.

You're afraid you'll make me cry
A reminder he's not here.
I know you cannot understand
And so I must be clear.

Please talk to me about him.
I want to hear his name.
I need to know you miss him
And your life is not the same.

Tell me how he made you laugh
Then tell me once again.
A school buddy or in the corps
Just start "I knew him when."

You see he's with me all the time,
Cannot forget he's gone,
Knowing you remember, too,
Will help me carry on.

GUILT

It interrupts your sleep at night,
And takes your breath away.
Will bring you to your knees in prayer,
Wants in your mind to stay.

Many bereaved parents it has plagued
Causing them to fear,
Question all they did and not for
A child no longer here.

There were times I clearly failed you
Since your death I've come to know.
I carried such a heavy load
You now know this is so.

I'm sorry for the games I missed,
And the times I wasn't there
To listen to the needs you had,
Not that I didn't care.

Are we punished with our child's death?
Such questions fill the mind.
And just as with the question *Why*
You'll not an answer find.

HOLIDAYS

POWERFUL DAYS

No matter what day of the week it is
For most, one's like another.
No triggers to bring up painful thoughts
When a father or a mother.

But certain days within the year
Prove all are not the same,
Evoking thoughts of children gone,
Powerful days that have a name.

One falls in May, another June.
Each year we search for ways
To remember with joy the reasons
For which mothers and fathers have days.

ANOTHER YEAR

~~~~~~

Another year begins
The calendar shows,
Twelve months start to finish
Then to a close.

But for many, the year
Runs a different course,
The trigger for change
An indescribable force.

We feel it before
We know that it's here.
The event that
Marks another year.

Our child, grandchild,
Or sibling gone,
Their death anniversary
Moves our time on.

I appreciate intent,
Kind wishes I hear.
And my calendar helps
Keep my mind clear.

"Before and after" his death
Now measure my time.
The clock of my heart
That speaks to my mind.

BEING THANKFUL

It's not easy being thankful
When you're no longer here.
It's not that I'm ungrateful, just
That death makes life unclear.

I'm thankful for a mind that still
Remembers you so well, and
The life we shared together
Left stories I can tell.

I'm thankful for the things I have,
Reminders of your life,
Childhood drawings, baseball cards,
Your writings, and Scout knife.

I'm thankful for all family
Now gone and those still here,
The many friends now in my life,
'Twas death that brought us near.

Why does this season cause me pain
When thankful for so much
And knowing you're still with me, simply
Out of sight and touch?

Please know I'm not ungrateful
If not up to holiday mirth
For I'm thankful that I shared the life
You lived when on this earth.

DID SHE KNOW?

The smell of pine trees in the air
Carols heard this time of year
I feel the difference deep inside
Christmas time is almost here.

My thoughts begin a journey
As I ponder stories told
Of another bereaved mother
Whose son did not grow old.

I wonder, now, was she aware
At the time her son was born
The limit on his earthly stay,
Life's fabric would be torn?

She was so young, how could she know
When cradling him new
That love could not protect them from
The pain they'd both go through?

I hope 'twas not within her mind,
The nightmare she would live
When his death would leave her empty
With nothing left to give.

These thoughts of her are new to me
Struggling with this test
Of facing Christmas once again
Since he was laid to rest.

HEALING

HOW ARE YOU?

~~~~~~~~~~~~~~~~~~~~~~~~~~~

I
am better,
like the tree that's
been stripped of its limbs
by fire begins new growth after
a period of time. Still rooted in the
same dirt, in the same location, with its
new growth appears to be the same tree; but
it's not. It has lived through a devastating blow that
has forever changed its core.

My Fate

How can you after all this time
Say you still miss him so?
Why not forget what could have been
And simply let him go?

Why have shelves of memories,
Reminders that he lived?
Why, when he died a man
Still think of him your kid?

Clearly you've gone on with life,
Know love and happiness,
Engaged in helping others
So why still reminisce?

These questions caused me pause
For how could I explain?
My son was so much more to me
Than photos and a name.

Yes, I've again found happiness,
Contented most the time.
I know what really matters,
Careful how I use my time.

My intent had never been
To build a shrine, you see.
I'd connect by phoning him
And sometimes he'd call me.

"Hi, Mom," he'd say. "It's Zach,"
Then talk about his day,
Giving me great comfort,
Knowing everything's OK.

In death as with his life
Part of me he'll always be.
Mementos soften the effects
Of stark reality.

His dreams and future are no more,
I can't participate.
Remembering his past upon
His death became my fate.

Lost and Found

How to explain it,
Explain to another,
The impact of loss on
The mind of a mother.

It happens so sudden,
This losing one's mind.
Much different than brain
Cells destroyed over time.

The moment you learn
That your child is dead
A lifetime of memories
Explode in your head.

And how do I now,
Using paper and pen
Explain how a lost mind
Can function again?

With effort the mind
Slowly opens back up,
Information pours in
As if filling a cup.

And the mind adapts,
It must keep us sane
As we carry on,
Though never the same.

Statistics

Every day throughout the world
A thousand times a day
Some almost have an accident
But they come through OK.

Patients on their deathbeds
Suddenly pull through,
Others with grave injuries
Are healed by something new.

Thousands of red lights are run,
And some with death do flirt.
Many times when chrome meets chrome
All walk away unhurt.

Now and then throughout the world
A near miss it is not,
Cars collide, someone dies, and
The world for many stops.

Finding the Quiet

Is it healing or numbness
I don't really know,
It's just that I'm grateful
To let the pain go.

Was it six years or eight
When the change took place?
When, with photo in hand,
I could smile at his face?

I no longer ponder
Just why he was sent.
We could all be part of
Some grand experiment.

He was here and I loved him
And held him to me.
And he'll rest in my heart
For all eternity.

TEN YEARS

Ten years past now,
Where have I been?
To hell and back
And over again.

No longer angry,
Calm has set in.
Or is it simply that
I'm out of wind?

Adapted to life
Without my child,
Grown used to pain
Once fierce, now mild.

Though still not able
To understand *why,*
Can share what I know
Helping others get by.

There were gifts given me
By my child while alive,
And I now know of gifts
I've received since he died.

True meaning of life
I'd not known before,
Inconceivable loss
Seemed to open a door.

And when my time comes
From this world I'm gone,
Hope to hear from my child
"You did good, Mom."

WHY I WRITE

Don't misunderstand
Why I still write and draw
About grief deeply felt,
Though no longer raw.

Years since being trapped
In the nightmarish hell
Newly bereaved parents
Know painfully well.

I write for others
Of healing to be.
Give hope when they feel
As if drowning at sea.

And a mind that for years
The words could not find
Is now clear and open,
No longer confined.

My poems of great loss,
They are what I've done,
Giving to others while
Remembering my son.

I WATCH THE BIRDS

Used to be I had no time
To sit and rest awhile.
No time to contemplate what
It is that makes me smile.

And then his death took all from me,
I could not comprehend
How joy could ever take the place
Of pain that would not end.

But gradually the darkness left
And in its place came light.
Life took on a different hue,
New dimension to my sight.

Now I marvel at the wonder
Of the sounds I never heard,
Taking pleasure in the small things
Now, I watch the birds.

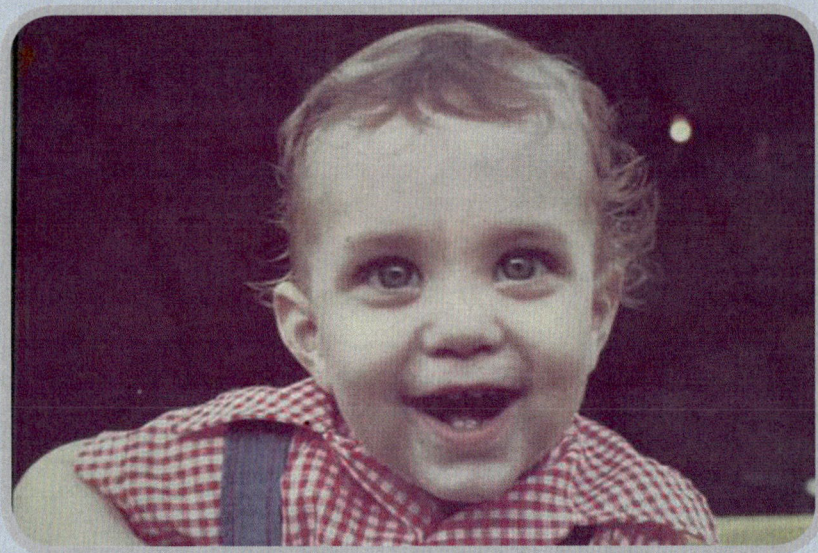

UNITED STATES MARINE CORPS
Company K, Third Battalion, Fourth Marines
UIC 39780
FPO AP 96609-9780

Georgia Ward
2152 Pacific Ave #B
Alameda, CA 94501

Dear Mrs. Ward

My name is Captain Sean Conley and I am your son's Commanding
Officer. I wanted to take the time to write you to let you know
what an outstanding Marine your son is. I do this because I
realize that many of our Marines, especially our top performers,
tend to downplay their achievements with others.

To say that Zachary is doing outstanding in the company would
be an understatement. He has recently been promoted to the rank
of Corporal, a Non-Commisisioned Officer in the Marine Corps.
That rank is not given out lightly in the infantry community in
which he works. It reflects a high degree of professionalism,
pride and dedication to the Marines in his unit. He has become a
leader within the company and this reflects the trust and
confidence that I have in his abilities and judgment. He has
helped his fellow Marines to adjust well and maintain positive
attitudes during the stressful time leading up to and during the
Okinawa deployment. He is a stellar example for the more junior
Marines to follow.

Your son has become an outstanding Marine due to the courage,
honor and commitment that he was obviously taught from a young
age. His actions and self sacrifice for the Corps and his country
are a great reflection of the values you instilled in him while
he was growing up. I am privileged to have been given the
opportunity to command such an outstanding Marine.

It certainly was my pleasure to communicate this good news to
you. You should be very proud of your son.

Semper Fidelis,

S.P. CONLEY
CAPT   USMC

37

38

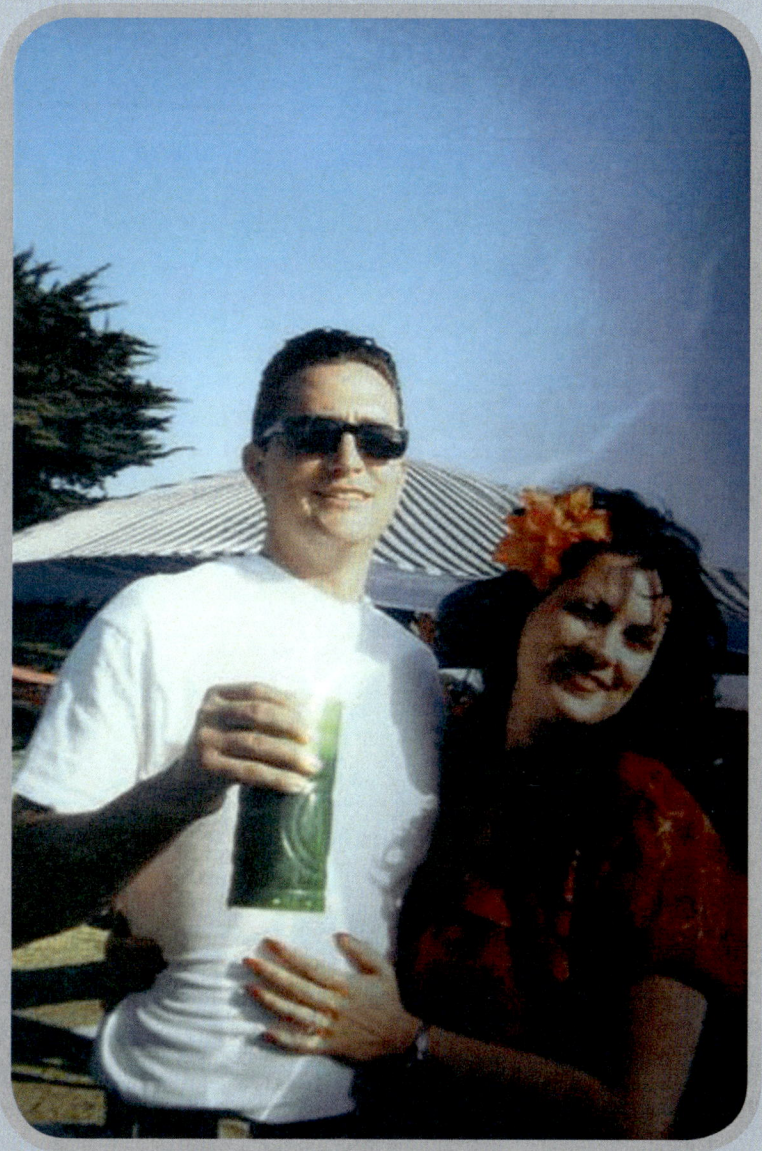

Both above photos are of Zach and Jessica.
Zach was killed on the date of their first-year wedding
anniversary.

Back row: Zach's stepdad Bruce Cockerham, Georgia, sister-in-law Patricia Ward, brother Aaron Ward.
Front row: Children of Aaron and Trish, Natalie, Kaden, and Rozlynn.

TCF CHAPTER LEADER AND MEETING FACILITATOR

~~~~~~~~~~~~~~~~~~~~~~~~

I dedicate these next two poems to all of the volunteer
TCF chapter meeting facilitators who, after receiving help
themselves,
provide compassion and hope to others.

Four months after Zach's accident, quickly spiraling down into a dark hole from which I could see no light, I realized that surviving my son's death required that I seek help. At the end of my first session, the counselor, a soft-spoken man, told me that I was clinically depressed. He said that he could help me with the depression but that he did not know what it is like to lose a child. He walked to a desk, wrote down a phone number, and while handing it to me said, "These people say they know." The phone number was for the national office of The Compassionate Friends, Inc.

THOSE WHO KNOW

The circle forms as each walks in.
Our monthly meeting gathers again.
Sorry for the reason we all are here
And grateful for an understanding ear.

We say our name and that of our child.
Share circumstances beyond our control.
At first—so hard to think and then talk.
Don't want to be here. Turn back the clock.

Deep grief, raw pain, all come seeking *why?*
Many ask why their child had to die.
The answer, we learn, is not to be found.
A simple question and yet so profound.

Inconceivable loss. Why did we not know
Our child could die before we would go?
Sitting together, we are *Those Who Know*.
Understanding your cry—"How can it be so?"

Here you'll find others among *Those Who Know*.
Navigating life broken—no longer whole.
As the amputee learns to move without limb,
We will help you to start living again.

As years go by, meetings come and go.
From our loss of one many more we now know.
Zach, Jessie, Sean, Kyle, Kevin, and Ron
Different ages and causes, but all now gone.

Lee, Steve, Sandy, Chase, McCaleb, and Jeff,
You guide us in helping those new to this test.
In remembering you we give what we can,
Believing that, someday, we'll hold you again.

The meetings helped us and we're here again,
As new bereaved parents in a fog walk in.
We are living proof that you will survive.
We are *Those Who Know*—our children have died.

OUT OF THE DARK

And when you've lost what I have,
Child, future, core part of me,
You know where the deepest darkness lies
No stranger to insanity.

Everything was gray at first,
A mantilla drawn across my face.
No color left upon this earth
In an instant gone without a trace.

Awoke each day to numbing pain,
All I knew without warning gone.
Needing to hear my child's voice again.
Death tugged at me, took strength to go on.

Like the sea stack rising mightily
From fog dissipating over the sea
Two years now painfully aware
His leaving this earth a finality.

Year three brought questions from others in pain
Hoping I'd answers to what could not be.
I spoke of my journey and how far I'd come
To anguished grievers listening to me.

And in the process of helping them
My gray veil lifted over time.
The trees and ocean took on hue
And I, again, could write and rhyme.

The change continued through year four
New awareness of what I could feel,
Spouse, grandkids, older son and wife,
Life in this changed world no longer surreal.

Five years since suffering the death of my child.
So different since what was me came undone.
No making sense of my child to be gone
When I'm growing old and he was so young.

Today when all light for others is lost,
And all they've known becomes cold and stark,
When the line 'tween sane and insanity's crossed,
I lift the gray veil, bring them Out of the Dark.

WRITING FOR FUN

A DAY WITH FRIENDS

I now take my days one at a time
Not knowing what each portends.
Whether feelings relay
A May day or Mayday,
Time's better when spent with my friends.

ALL IN A LIFE

~~~~~~~~~~~~~~~~~~~~~~~~~~~~~~~~

Life is a series of ups and downs,
Hills and valleys, smiles and frowns.

Ebbs and flows, highs and lows,
When life becomes fickle anything goes.

One day is sunny the next rain falls
A promising start then throws a curveball.

Age brings acceptance that both peace and strife
Are part of existing when living one's life.

The Bread Song
(Remembering Zach)

"Sing the bread song, Mom," he asked of me,
A two-year-old upon my knee.
"The bread song?" I asked questioning.
"I'm afraid I don't know what you mean."

"The bread song, Mom, please," he said
And the nightly songs went through my head.
"Is it 'Animal Crackers' or 'Close to You'?"
He shook his head "no"—they wouldn't do.

"Can't think of a bread song," shrugging to him.
"You know it, Mom, please sing it again."
So I thought of another and asked, "'Do Re Me'?"
"That's the one, Mom," he squealed gleefully.

Above photo of Zach is from the book *Broken Down Heroes* by Jay Watson.

Zach and Georgia